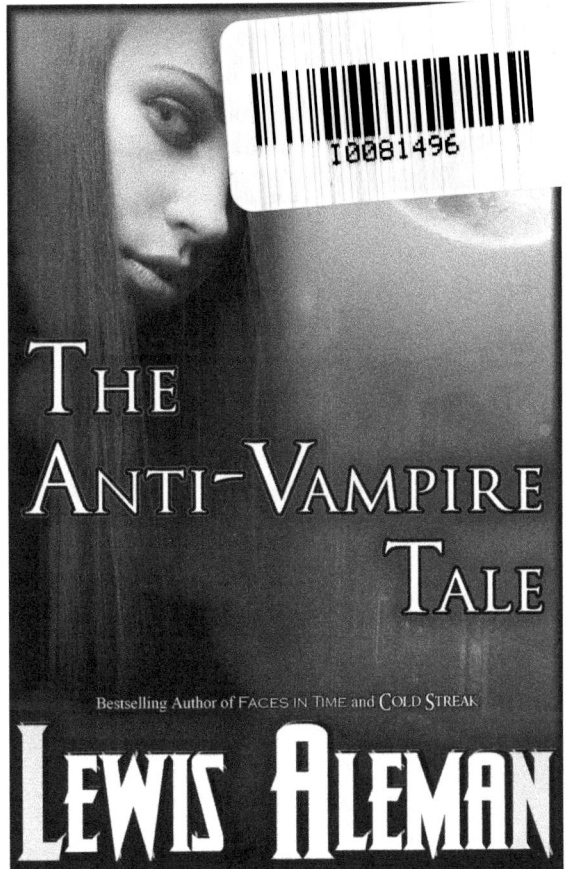

PEYTON MANNING

& THE DENVER BRONCOS

*THE COMEBACK
5,477 YARDS,
55 TDs,
& HIS RETURN TO
THE SUPERBOWL*

Dan Fathow

MEGALODON ENTERTAINMENT, LLC.

Published by Megalodon Entertainment, LLC. (USA)
www.MegalodonEntertainment.com

First Printing: February 2014

Printed in the United States of America.

ISBN: 978-1-61589-043-9
ISBN-10: 1-61589-043-2

BULK INQUERIES:
Quantity discounts are available on bulk orders of this novel for educational, fund-raising, promotional, and special sales purposes.
For details, please contact www.MegalodonEntertainment.com

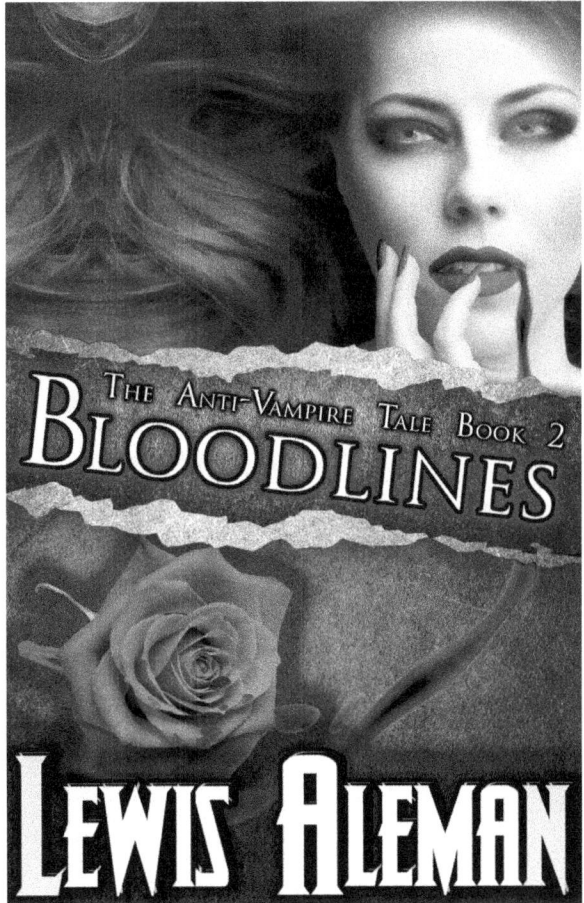

PEYTON MANNING

& THE DENVER BRONCOS

THE COMEBACK 5,477 YARDS, 55 TDs, & HIS RETURN TO THE SUPERBOWL

Dan Fathow

MEGALODON ENTERTAINMENT, LLC.

TABLE OF CONTENTS

PART I: 2013 AFC CHAMPIONSHIP SEASON

PART II: SUPER BOWL XLVIII MATCHUP VS. THE SEAHAWKS.... 99

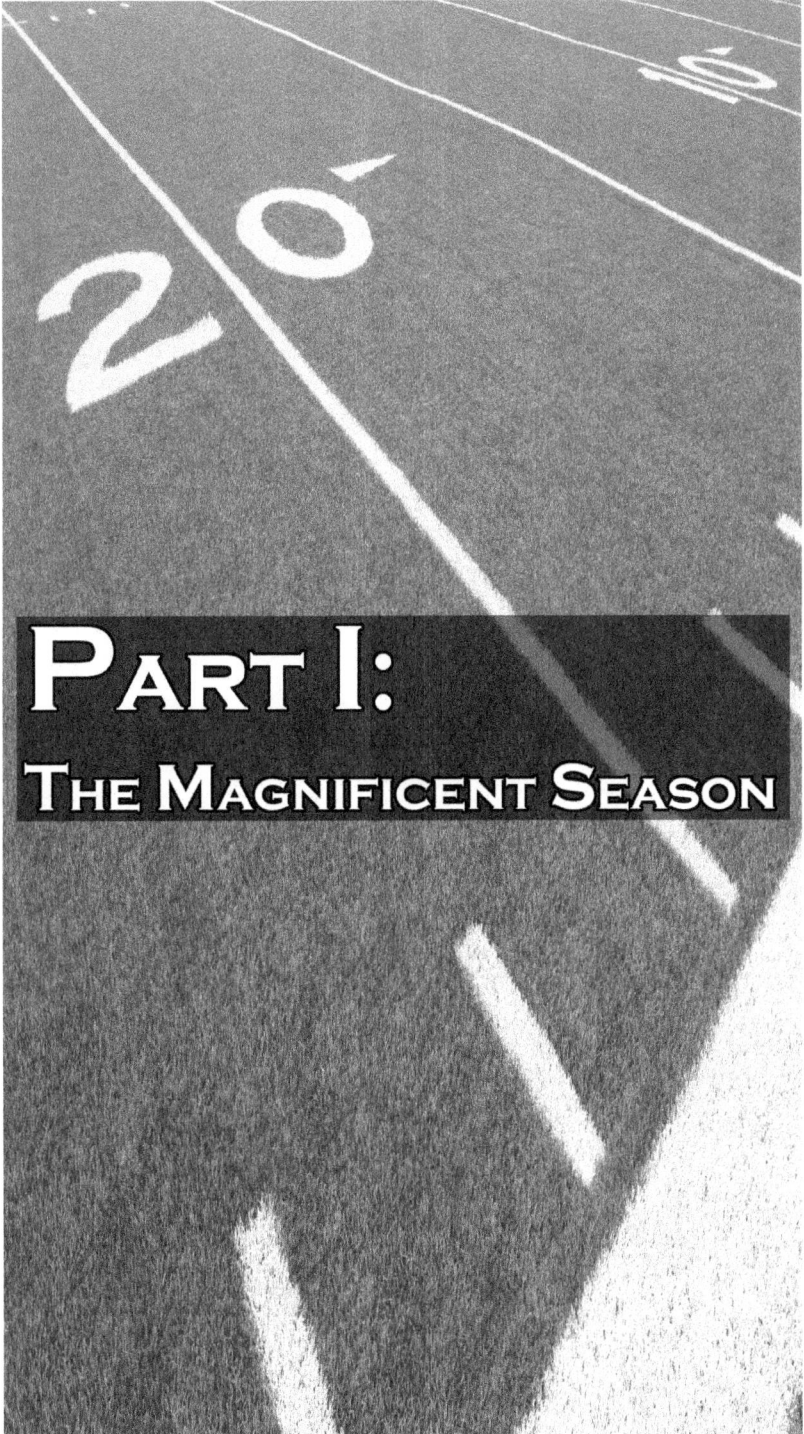

PART I:
THE MAGNIFICENT SEASON

WEEK 1

September 5, 2013
Sports Authority Field – Mile High, Denver, CO

Teams	1st	2nd	3rd	4th	Total
Baltimore Ravens	7	10	0	10	27
Denver Broncos	0	14	21	14	49

GAME SUMMARY

The opening game of the Denver Broncos' 2013 season presented them with the daunting task of playing the reigning Super Bowl Champion Baltimore Ravens. There isn't a much harder task in all of football.

The first half was a competitive, close contest, as Joe Flacco and the Ravens put up a touchdown in the first quarter to take the lead of 7-0. In the second quarter, The Ravens put up another touchdown and a field goal, but the Broncos would fight right back with 2 touchdowns of their own. At halftime, the Super Bowl champs were 3 points ahead of Denver with a score of 17-14, which is what most experts would have expected in this contest.

The second half was a completely different story, and an exciting one for Broncos fans. Peyton Manning really set the tone for the season, starting the second half with all guns blazing, throwing for 3 touchdowns and giving his team a cushy 35-17 lead.

Baltimore bounced back somewhat in the 4th quarter scoring a touchdown and a field goal of their own, but Denver would not be outdone, scoring 2 additional touchdowns. For those keeping score, that's 7 touchdowns for Peyton Manning in the season opener. Yes, 7.

While the Ravens didn't play poorly by putting up 27 points against the Broncos and leading the game at the half, they were simply outplayed and dominated in the second half. While the final score was 49-27, the second half score was even more impressive at 35-10.

Manning didn't get a lot of help on the ground; the team combined accounted for only 65 rushing yards and 0 touchdowns.

In the air, Manning's favorite targets were the 2 Thomas's, Demaryius and Julius, who both caught for over 100 yards with 2 TDs a piece. Denver's next most productive receiver was Wes Welker, who also had 9 grabs for 67 yards and 2 TDs. The 7th passing touchdown of the game was caught by Andre Caldwell in his only grab of the day.

The all-important turnover war was even with the Ravens throwing 2 interceptions and the Broncos losing 2 fumbles.

462-yards was the damage inflicted upon the Ravens by Manning's arm. He threw 7 touchdowns while connecting on 27 of 42 passes and achieving a remarkable 141 RTG and 83.6 Quarterback Rating. What's even more impressive is that he was able to accomplish this against a good opponent, while being sacked 3 times, and giving up 0 interceptions. All of the above statistics are remarkable and truly set the tone for the Broncos' 2013 season. Establishing dominance so early on is a huge psychological advantage for any team.

TEAM LEADERS

Passing

Peyton Manning #18
462 Yards, 7 Touchdowns, 0 Interceptions
(27/42, 64.3 Comp %)

Rushing

Knowshon Moreno #27
28 Yards on 9 Carries
3.11 Yards per Carry
0 Rushing Touchdowns

Montee Ball #28
24 Yards on 8 Carries
3.00 Yards per Carry
0 Rushing Touchdowns

Receiving

Demaryius Thomas #88
161 Yards on 5 Receptions
32.20 Yards per Reception
2 Touchdown Receptions

Julius Thomas #80
110 Yards on 5 Receptions
22.00 Yards per Reception

2 Touchdown Receptions

Wes Welker #83
67 Yards on 9 Receptions
7.44 Yards per Reception
2 Touchdown Receptions

Knowshon Moreno #27
37 Yards on 3 Receptions
12.33 Yards per Reception
0 Touchdown Receptions

Andre Caldwell #12
28 Yards on 1 Reception
28.00 Yards per Reception
1 Touchdown Reception

Kicking

Matt Prater #5
7 Points Total
0/0 Field Goals
7/7 Extra Points

Interceptions

Danny Trevathan #59
1 Interception

Chris Harris #25
1 Interception

MANNING CANNON COUNT

MANNING CANNON COUNT

IN PURSUIT OF HISTORY

7  **462**

TOUCHDOWNS | **YARDS**

AFTER **1** GAME

THE BOTTOM LINE

THE BOTTOM LINE

1 - 0

WEEK 2

September 15, 2013
Met Life Stadium – East Rutherford, NJ

Teams	1st	2nd	3rd	4th	Total
Denver Broncos	0	10	14	17	**41**
New York Giants	3	6	7	7	**23**

GAME SUMMARY

"Manning Versus Manning" and "The Manning Bowl" was how the second game of the Broncos' season was touted, as Peyton faced off against Eli on the Giant's home turf in New Jersey.

The Ney York Giants had gotten off to a rough start that would be just as indicative of bad things to come as the Broncos' fantastic start was to their great season. In the previous week's contest, Eli Manning threw for an impressive 450 yards and 4 TDs, but their undoing was also linked to his performance, which included 3 Interceptions.

Also in the prior week's game, the Giants' leading rusher only accounted for 23 yards, while the team's total rushing stats were a meager 50 yards and 0 Touchdowns. So, he certainly wasn't getting much help on the ground.

Okay, so Week 1 showed us a very impressive victory for the Broncos and an inconsistent loss for the Giants.

So, what did that translate to in Week 2?

Very good news for the Broncos. Very bad news for the Giants.

With a lopsided final score of 41-23, it's a bit hard to believe the score at the end of the first quarter was 3-0 in favor of the Giants. Even the score at the half is a head-scratcher as Denver only led by 1 point, 10-9. Much like the first game of the season, Peyton Manning came out of halftime slinging the football like no one else. First half – 10 points. Second Half - 31 points. Scoring 3 times as many points in the second half as the first is something to note, as it can be a strength and a weakness. Consistent football is always the goal from first snap to final play, but there's hardly any denying that the Broncos were manhandling their opponents thus far, regardless of how unevenly the points were being scored.

The first half was pretty evenly played. What changed in the second half? Eli Manning threw for an impressive 362 yards, but he only threw for 1 touchdown and tossed away an astonishing 4 interceptions. By contrast, Peyton Manning threw for slightly less yards at 307 with 2 TDs and 0 Interceptions. Slightly less yards with 4 less turnovers and twice as many touchdowns will nearly always equal victory, if not an all-out trouncing, which is what happened here.

One of the big improvements from the previous week was in Denver's running game. It accounted for 107 yards and 2 TDs, mostly due to the work of Knowshon Marino who carried 13 times for 93 yards and both of the team's rushing TDs.

This also marked the second week in a row that cornerback Chris Harris nabbed an interception.

While Peyton's numbers were not quite as good as the previous week's stats, he led his team to an equally impressive victory. He was 30 for 43 passes for 307 yards with 2 TDs and 0 Interceptions, with a QBR of 89.1 and RTG of 105.5. His completion percentage was an impressive 69.8, which was much better than his fraternal opponent's 57.1 completion percentage.

TEAM LEADERS

Passing

Peyton Manning #18
307 Yards, 2 Touchdowns, 0 Interceptions
(30/43, 69.76 Comp %)

Rushing

Knowshon Moreno #27
93 Yards on 13 Carries
7.15 Yards per Carry
2 Rushing Touchdowns

Montee Ball #28
14 Yards on 12 Carries
1.17 Yards per Carry
0 Rushing Touchdowns

Receiving

Eric Decker #87
87 Yards on 9 Receptions
9.67 Yards per Reception
0 Touchdown Receptions

Demaryius Thomas #88
52 Yards on 5 Receptions
10.4 Yards per Reception
0 Touchdown Receptions

Julius Thomas #80
47 Yards on 6 Receptions
7.83 Yards per Reception
1 Touchdown Reception

Wes Welker #83
39 Yards on 3 Receptions
13.00 Yards per Reception
1 Touchdown Reception

Andre Caldwell #12
36 Yards on 1 Reception
36.00 Yards per Reception
0 Touchdown Receptions

Kicking

Matt Prater #5
11 Points Total
2/2 Field Goals
5/5 Extra Points

Interceptions

Chris Harris #25
1 Interception

Tony Carter #32
1 Interception

Rahim Moore #26
1 Interception

Dominique Rodgers-Cromartie #45
1 Interception

MANNING CANNON COUNT

IN PURSUIT OF HISTORY

9 | 769

TOUCHDOWNS | **YARDS**

AFTER **2** GAMES

THE BOTTOM LINE

2 - 0

WEEK 3

September 23, 2013
Sports Authority Field – Mile High, Denver, CO

Teams	1st	2nd	3rd	4th	Total
Oakland Raiders	0	7	7	7	21
Denver Broncos	10	17	3	7	37

GAME SUMMARY

Week 3 had the 2-0 Broncos facing the 1-1 Oakland Raiders. In the previous 2 games, the Oakland Raiders scored 36 points while allowing opponents to score 30. On the other hand, the Broncos more than doubled that by scoring 90 points while allowing opponents to score 50. Even though the Broncos allowed 20 more points to their opponents than the Raiders did to their competition, Denver outscored their opposition by a whopping 40 points (20 points a game), while the Raiders only outscored their opposition by 6 points (3 points a game). Clearly, the Broncos were the favorites in this contest.

So far in the NFL Season, the only criticism one could reasonably bring against Peyton Manning and the Denver Broncos' offense was that they were slow-starting. The Broncos had yet to get on the scoreboard in the first quarter of their first two games. In fact, more than half of Denver's points had been scored in the second half of their previous games.

Peyton Manning had another banner day, throwing for 374 yards, 3 touchdowns, and 0 interceptions. As strong as those numbers are, perhaps the most telling stat of the day was Manning accomplished this completing 32 of 37 passes for a remarkable 86.49 completion percentage.

TEAM LEADERS

Passing

Peyton Manning #18
374 Yards, 3 Touchdown, 0 Interceptions
(32/37, 86.49 Comp %)

Rushing

Ronnie Hillman #21
66 Yards on 9 Carries
7.33 Yards per Carry
1 Rushing Touchdown

Montee Ball #28
61 Yards on 11 Carries
5.55 Yards per Carry
0 Rushing Touchdowns

Knowshon Moreno #27
39 Yards on 12 Carries
3.25 Yards per Carry
0 Rushing Touchdowns

Receiving

Eric Decker #87
133 Yards on 8 Receptions
16.63 Yards per Reception
1 Touchdown Reception

Demaryius Thomas #88
94 Yards on 10 Receptions
9.40 Yards per Reception
0 Touchdown Receptions

Wes Welker #83
84 Yards on 7 Receptions
12.00 Yards per Reception
1 Touchdown Reception

Julius Thomas #80
37 Yards on 3 Receptions
12.33 Yards per Reception
1 Touchdown Reception

Kicking

Matt Prater #5
13 Points Total
3/3 Field Goals
4/4 Extra Points

Interceptions

None

MANNING CANNON COUNT

IN PURSUIT OF HISTORY

12 | 1,143

TOUCHDOWNS | YARDS

AFTER 3 GAMES

THE BOTTOM LINE

3 - 0

WEEK 4

September 29, 2013
Sports Authority Field – Mile High, Denver, CO

Teams	1st	2nd	3rd	4th	Total
Philadelphia Eagles	3	10	0	7	**20**
Denver Broncos	14	7	21	10	**52**

GAME SUMMARY

In Week 4, the Eagles were 1-2 and not off to a great start. The team did however have potential that was later demonstrated by winning 7 of their last 8 games and earning a wild card playoff berth.

Total offensive yards were similar for both teams despite the score. Denver had 22 more yards with 472 with the Eagles trailing at 450.

The game was also free of turnovers for both teams.

So with total offense being so similar and no turnovers, what made this game a 32-point blowout?

There were a few factors that contributed to the differential. Possibly the most likely culprit was red zone efficiency. Denver was perfect in the red zone, going 5 for 5, but Philadelphia was only 2 for 5. Being able to capitalize 2 and a half times more than your opponent in the red zone is typically going to equal victory. In addition, the Broncos' Special Teams also contributed greatly with 2 touchdowns of their own; Philadelphia had none. Another contributing factor was that Denver was sacked only once while Philadelphia was sacked 3 times.

The play of the game, if not the entire week, was easily Trindon Holliday's amazing 105-yard kickoff return for a touchdown.

Worthy of note was the performance of kicker Matt Prater, who was perfect through 4 games, accounting for 41of the Broncos' points thus far in the season.

Peyton Manning had another 300+ yard game, throwing for 327 yards, 4 touchdowns, and 0 interceptions. He connected on 28 of 34 passes for an 82.35 completion percentage.

TEAM LEADERS

Passing

Peyton Manning #18
327 Yards, 4 Touchdowns, 0 Interceptions
(28/34, Comp 82.35 %)

Brock Osweiler #17
10 Yards, 0 Touchdowns, 0 Interceptions
(2/3, Comp 66.67 %)

Rushing

Knowshon Moreno #27
78 Yards on 12 Carries
6.50 Yards per Carry
1 Rushing Touchdown

Ronnie Hillman #21
36 Yards on 11 Carries
3.27 Yards per Carry
0 Rushing Touchdowns

Montee Ball #28
24 Yards on 8 Carries
3.00 Yards per Carry
0 Rushing Touchdowns

Receiving

Eric Decker #87
88 Yards on 5 Receptions
17.60 Yards per Reception
0 Touchdown Receptions

Demaryius Thomas #88
86 Yards on 9 Receptions
9.56 Yards per Reception
2 Touchdown Receptions

Wes Welker #83
76 Yards on 7 Receptions
10.86 Yards per Reception
2 Touchdown Receptions

Julius Thomas #80
43 Yards on 4 Receptions
10.75 Yards per Reception
0 Touchdown Receptions

Kicking

Matt Prater #5
10 Points Total
1/1 Field Goals
7/7 Extra Points

Interceptions

None

MANNING CANNON COUNT

IN PURSUIT OF HISTORY

16 | 1,470

TOUCHDOWNS | **YARDS**

AFTER **4** GAMES

THE BOTTOM LINE

4 - 0

WEEK 5

October 6, 2013
Sports Authority Field – Mile High, Denver, CO

Teams	1st	2nd	3rd	4th	Total
Denver Broncos	7	21	10	13	**51**
Dallas Cowboys	14	6	13	15	**48**

GAME SUMMARY

Week 5 saw the Broncos going to Arlington, Texas to duel the Cowboys. Going into Week 5, the Broncos were undefeated at 4-0, and the Cowboys were struggling to maintain .500 at 2-2. What was deceptive about Dallas was that they were 2-0 at home, and this game was at AT&T Stadium.

Not many people were expecting the 99-point offensive tug-of-war that took place, but it proved to be the game to watch that week, along with being the Broncos' unexpectedly toughest test thus far in the season.

Peyton Manning had a great day connecting on 33 of 42 passes for 414 yards, 4 touchdowns, and 1 interception (his first of the season). A 78.57 completion percentage was certainly hard to beat.

Manning's gunslinging opponent, Tony Romo, had a mixed bag of a day. He actually out-threw future hall-of-famer Manning by nearly 100 yards with an impressive 506 yards on 25 of 36 passes for a 69.44 completion percentage. He also had

5 touchdowns, one more than Manning, but his 4th quarter interception came during a possible game-winning drive, unfortunately adding to Romo's legacy of ill-timed interceptions that lost the Cowboys key games.

Romo did not get a lot of help in this contest as he was sacked 4 times while Manning was not sacked at all. His team's run game was anemic, as it accounted for only 52 yards total, 7 of them coming from Romo himself. Dallas had 9 penalties for 81 yards, while Denver only had 5 flags for 55 yards. On these costly penalties, Denver received 5 first downs.

Knowshon Moreno had a fantastic day putting up 150 yards total on the ground and in the air and a touchdown. On rushing alone, he racked up 93 yards, which was nearly double the yardage that the entire Cowboys offense was able to run.

TEAM LEADERS

Passing

Peyton Manning #18
414 Yards, 4 Touchdowns, 1 Interception
(33/42, Comp 78.57 %)

Rushing

Knowshon Moreno #27
93 Yards on 19 Carries
4.89 Yards per Carry
1 Rushing Touchdown

Ronnie Hillman #21
17 Yards on 7 Carries
2.43 Yards per Carry
0 Rushing Touchdowns

Montee Ball #28
1 Yards on 1 Carries
1.00 Yards per Carry
0 Rushing Touchdowns

Receiving

Julius Thomas #80
122 Yards on 9 Receptions
13.56 Yards per Reception
2 Touchdown Receptions

Eric Decker #87
87 Yards on 5 Receptions
17.40 Yards per Reception
0 Touchdown Receptions

Knowshon Moreno #27
57 Yards on 5 Receptions
11.40 Yards per Reception
2 Touchdown Receptions

Demaryius Thomas #88
57 Yards on 5 Receptions
11.40 Yards per Reception
0 Touchdown Receptions

Wes Welker #83
49 Yards on 5 Receptions
9.80 Yards per Reception
1 Touchdown Reception

Kicking

Matt Prater #5
15 Points Total
3/3 Field Goals
6/6 Extra Points

Interceptions

Danny Trevathan #59
1 Interception

MANNING CANNON COUNT

IN PURSUIT OF HISTORY

20 | 1,884

TOUCHDOWNS | YARDS

AFTER 5 GAMES

THE BOTTOM LINE

5 - 0

WEEK 6

October 13, 2013
Sports Authority Field – Mile High, Denver, CO

Teams	1st	2nd	3rd	4th	Total
Jacksonville Jaguars	0	12	7	0	19
Denver Broncos	14	0	14	7	35

GAME SUMMARY

The Jaguars and the Broncos were polar opposites coming into this game. Denver was undefeated and already a favorite to reach the Super Bowl. On the other side, the Jaguars were 0-5, having yet to win a single game and needing nothing short of winning almost all of their remaining games just to make the playoffs.

The final score was a 16-point victory for the Broncos, which was to be expected. What was not to be expected was that Chad Henne barely edged out Manning for most passing yards, by throwing 303 to Peyton's 295. In fact, it became the first game of the season in which Manning did not throw for at least 300 yards. The bigger difference between the 2 quarterbacks came in the form of Manning throwing for 2 touchdowns and 0 interceptions, while Henne threw for 0 touchdowns and 2 interceptions. However, Manning did fumble the ball twice, losing it both times to the Jaguars.

Once again, Knowshon Moreno contributed a great deal to this win. On the ground, he was the top performer with 42 yards and 3 touchdowns. In the air, he had 3 grabs for an additional 62 yards.

Manning's 295 yards may have been his lowest numbers so far in the year, but they were still great, especially when they came on a 66.67 completion ratio, 2 touchdowns, and a 6-0 record.

TEAM LEADERS

Passing

Peyton Manning #18
295 Yards, 2 Touchdowns, 1 Interception
(28/42, 66.67 Comp %)

Rushing

Knowshon Moreno #27
42 Yards on 15 Carries
2.8 Yards per Carry
3 Rushing Touchdowns

David Bruton #30
35 Yards on 1 Carries
35.00 Yards per Carry
0 Rushing Touchdowns

Ronnie Hillman #21
20 Yards on 4 Carries
5.00 Yards per Carry
0 Rushing Touchdowns

Montee Ball #28
15 Yards on 3 Carries
5.00 Yards per Carry
0 Rushing Touchdowns

Receiving

Demaryius Thomas #88
78 Yards on 3 Receptions
26.00 Yards per Reception
0 Touchdown Receptions

Wes Welker #83
63 Yards on 6 Receptions
10.50 Yards per Reception
1 Touchdown Reception

Knowshon Moreno #27
62 Yards on 7 Receptions
8.86 Yards per Reception
0 Touchdown Receptions

Eric Decker #87
50 Yards on 5 Receptions
10.00 Yards per Reception
0 Touchdown Receptions

Julius Thomas #80
22 Yards on 4 Receptions
5.50 Yards per Reception
1 Touchdown Reception

Kicking

Matt Prater #5
5 Points Total
0/0 Field Goals
5/5 Extra Points

Interceptions

Danny Trevathan #59
1 Interception

Kayvon Webster #36
1 Interception

MANNING CANNON COUNT

IN PURSUIT OF HISTORY

22
TOUCHDOWNS

2,179
YARDS

AFTER 6 GAMES

THE BOTTOM LINE

THE BOTTOM LINE

6 - 0

WEEK 7

October 20, 2013
Lucas Oil Stadium, Indianapolis, IN

Teams	1st	2nd	3rd	4th	Total
Denver Broncos	7	7	3	16	**33**
Indianapolis Colts	10	16	7	6	**39**

GAME SUMMARY

Upset is the only word to describe this contest. Even before the first snap, it had the setting of a great action/drama battle. Peyton Manning was returning to Indianapolis for the first time to battle his old team, the team that decided to move on without him following his injury. He was the comeback kid, returning to his old battlefield for retribution.

The Indianapolis Colts were certainly not having a poor season, as they were 4-2, coming into the game with a 2-1 home record. While those numbers were promising, they paled in comparison to the undefeated Denver Broncos.

As often decides professional football outcomes, the turnover battle was highly influential in this game. The Broncos in uncharacteristic fashion gave up 3 turnovers in the form of 2 lost fumbles and 1 interception. Conversely, the Colts only gave up 1 fumble.

Peyton Manning had a great day, despite the loss, throwing for 386 yards, 3 touchdowns, and 1 interception. What was even more impressive was that he achieved this while being sacked 4 times. Manning did not have a tremendous amount of support on the ground. The Broncos only rushed for 64 yards, although Moreno did run in another touchdown.

Eric Decker had a fantastic day catching 8 receptions for 150 yards and 1 touchdown. Wes Welker also had nearly 100 receiving yards. In addition, both of the Thomases had receiving touchdowns in this game.

TEAM LEADERS

Passing

Peyton Manning #18
386 Yards, 3 Touchdowns, 1 Interception
(29/49, 59.18 Comp %)

Rushing

Knowshon Moreno #27
40 Yards on 15 Carries
2.67 Yards per Carry
1 Rushing Touchdown

Ronnie Hillman #21
25 Yards on 4 Carries
6.25 Yards per Carry
0 Rushing Touchdowns

Receiving

Eric Decker #87
150 Yards on 8 Receptions
18.75 Yards per Reception
1 Touchdown Receptions

Wes Welker #83
96 Yards on 7 Receptions
13.71 Yards per Reception
0 Touchdown Reception

Demaryius Thomas #88
82 Yards on 4 Receptions
20.5 Yards per Reception
1 Touchdown Receptions

Julius Thomas #80
41 Yards on 5 Receptions
8.20 Yards per Reception
1 Touchdown Receptions

Knowshon Moreno #27
9 Yards on 3 Receptions
3.00 Yards per Reception
0 Touchdown Receptions

Kicking

Matt Prater #5
9 Points Total
2/2 Field Goals
3/3 Extra Points

Interceptions

None

MANNING CANNON COUNT

IN PURSUIT OF HISTORY

25		2,565
TOUCHDOWNS		YARDS

AFTER **7** GAMES

THE BOTTOM LINE

6 - 1

WEEK 8

October 27, 2013
Sports Authority Field – Mile High, Denver, CO

Teams	1st	2nd	3rd	4th	Total
Washington Redskins	0	7	14	0	**21**
Denver Broncos	7	0	7	31	**45**

GAME SUMMARY

Coming off their unexpected Week 7 loss to the Colts on the road, the Broncos had something to prove meeting the Redskins at home the following week.

Washington was already having a disappointing year, having fallen to a 2-4 record. The team was not playing well overall, and Robert Griffin III was not performing up to the expectations of some. He'd eventually finish the year with 3,203 passing yards, a 60% completion percentage, 16 touchdowns, and 12 interceptions.

Unfortunately for Redskins fans, they were facing off against a team having a great year with a hot quarterback having a record-breaking season.

Peyton Manning had a mixed day as he threw for 354 yards on 30 of 44 passes for 4 touchdowns. The downside was he had nearly as many interceptions with 3. He was sacked twice in this contest, but he still led his team to victory and managed to maintain a 68.18 completion percentage.

Knowshon Moreno once again was the biggest contributor to the Peyton-Manning-led offense as he was both the team's leading rusher and second-leading receiver, racking up a total of 132 yards and 1 touchdown.

Wes Welker had a great day too, catching 6 passes for 81 yards and a TD.

The Denver defense gave Manning and the offense a lot of help in this one, nabbing 4 of RG3's passes for interceptions, including 1 of them being returned for a touchdown.

TEAM LEADERS

Passing

Peyton Manning #18
354 Yards, 4 Touchdowns, 3 Interceptions
(30/44, 68.18 Comp %)

Rushing

Knowshon Moreno #27
43 Yards on 13 Carries
3.31 Yards per Carry
0 Rushing Touchdowns

Montee Ball #28
38 Yards on 12 Carries
3.17 Yards per Carry
1 Rushing Touchdown

Ronnie Hillman #21
22 Yards on 4 Carries
5.50 Yards per Carry

0 Rushing Touchdowns

Receiving

Julius Thomas #80
122 Yards on 9 Receptions
13.56 Yards per Reception
2 Touchdown Receptions

Knowshon Moreno #27
89 Yards on 6 Receptions
14.83 Yards per Reception
1 Touchdown Reception

Eric Decker #87
87 Yards on 5 Receptions
17.40 Yards per Reception
0 Touchdown Receptions

Demaryius Thomas #88
57 Yards on 5 Receptions
11.40 Yards per Reception
0 Touchdown Receptions

Wes Welker #83
49 Yards on 5 Receptions
9.80 Yards per Reception
1 Touchdown Reception

Kicking

Matt Prater #5
9 Points Total
1/1 Field Goals

PEYTON MANNING 48

6/6 Extra Points

Interceptions

Chris Harris #25
1 Interception

Shaun Phillips #90
1 Interception

Rahim Moore #26
1 Interception

Dominique Rodgers-Cromartie #45
1 Interception Returned for a Touchdown

MANNING CANNON COUNT

IN PURSUIT OF HISTORY

29 | 2,919
TOUCHDOWNS | YARDS

AFTER **8** GAMES

THE BOTTOM LINE

6 - 2

WEEK 10

November 10, 2013
Qualcomm Stadium – San Diego, CA

Teams	1st	2nd	3rd	4th	Total
Denver Broncos	7	14	7	0	**28**
San Diego Chargers	0	6	7	7	**20**

GAME SUMMARY

Coming off a bye week, Peyton Manning and the Denver Broncos were facing the San Diego Chargers on the road.

Entering this game, the Chargers appeared to be grossly outmatched as they were struggling to tread water with a season record of 4-4. The Broncos were 7-1, having nearly twice as many victories with only a fourth as many losses. What those statistics did not show was the Chargers were an improving team that was just beginning to get it all together. The Chargers would end the regular season with a 9-7 record, winning the Wild Card game against the Bengals, and eventually facing the Broncos in the Divisional Championship.

In short, the Chargers were a better team than their record suggested, which was likely why this ended up being only an 8-point, 1-score (with 2-point conversion) game.

Peyton Manning grossly outperformed the Chargers' counterpart, Philip Rivers. Manning threw for 330 yards, 4 touchdowns, and 0 interceptions on 25 of 36 passes for a completion percentage of 69.44. Rivers threw for 218 yards, 1 touchdown, and 0 interceptions on 19 of 29 passes for a 65.52 completion percentage. Clearly, Manning dominated in every category, except they both did a great job of ball control, neither throwing a single interception.

Demaryius Thomas was on fire in this game, catching 7 passes for 108 yards and 3 touchdowns. Julius Thomas also had a great day, grabbing 3 passes for 96 yards and a TD.

TEAM LEADERS

Passing

Peyton Manning #18
330 Yards, 4 Touchdowns, 0 Interceptions
(25/36, 69.44 Comp %)

Rushing

Knowshon Moreno #27
65 Yards on 15 Carries
4.33 Yards per Carry
0 Rushing Touchdowns

Montee Ball #28
20 Yards on 5 Carries
4.00 Yards per Carry
0 Rushing Touchdowns

Receiving

Demaryius Thomas #88
108 Yards on 7 Receptions
11.40 Yards per Reception
3 Touchdown Receptions

Julius Thomas #80
96 Yards on 3 Receptions
32 Yards per Reception
1 Touchdown Reception

Eric Decker #87
52 Yards on 3 Receptions
17.33 Yards per Reception
0 Touchdown Receptions

Knowshon Moreno #27
49 Yards on 8 Receptions
6.13 Yards per Reception
0 Touchdown Receptions

Wes Welker #83
21 Yards on 3 Receptions
7.00 Yards per Reception
0 Touchdown Receptions

Kicking

Matt Prater #5
4 Points Total
0/0 Field Goals
4/4 Extra Points

Interceptions

MANNING CANNON COUNT

IN PURSUIT OF HISTORY

33 | **3,249**

TOUCHDOWNS | **YARDS**

AFTER **9** GAMES

THE BOTTOM LINE

8 - 1

WEEK 11

November 17, 2013
Sports Authority Field – Mile High, Denver, CO

Teams	1st	2nd	3rd	4th	Total
Kansas City Chiefs	0	10	0	7	**17**
Denver Broncos	10	7	7	3	**27**

GAME SUMMARY

The Kansas City Chiefs were 9-0 coming into this game, facing the 8-1 Denver Broncos. With a combined record of 17-1 between the 2 teams, it was definitely the game people were watching most in Week 11.

Peyton Manning had a strong day, racking up 323 passing yards, 1 touchdown, and 0 interceptions on 24 of 40 passes.

On the rushing front, Montee Ball had 2 rushing touchdowns. In the air, Demaryius Thomas was the man of the day catching 5 passes for 121 yards, one of them being a 70-yard reception.

Kicker Matt Prater had been absolutely perfect this season until finally missing a field goal in this game in which he was 2 for 3 on field goals and 3 for 3 on extra points.

TEAM LEADERS

Passing

Peyton Manning #18
323 Yards, 1 Touchdown, 0 Interceptions
(24/40, 60 Comp %)

Rushing

Knowshon Moreno #27
79 Yards on 27 Carries
2.93 Yards per Carry
0 Rushing Touchdowns

Montee Ball #28
25 Yards on 8 Carries
3.13 Yards per Carry
2 Rushing Touchdowns

Receiving

Demaryius Thomas #88
121 Yards on 5 Receptions
24.20 Yards per Reception
0 Touchdown Receptions

Wes Welker #83
72 Yards on 8 Receptions
9.00 Yards per Reception

0 Touchdown Receptions

Eric Decker #87
71 Yards on 5 Receptions
14.20 Yards per Reception
0 Touchdown Receptions

Julius Thomas #80
43 Yards on 3 Receptions
14.33 Yards per Reception
1 Touchdown Reception

Kicking

Matt Prater #5
9 Points Total
2/3 Field Goals
3/3 Extra Points

Interceptions

None

MANNING CANNON COUNT

MANNING CANNON COUNT

IN PURSUIT OF HISTORY

34 | 3,572

TOUCHDOWNS | YARDS

AFTER 10 GAMES

THE BOTTOM LINE

9 - 1

WEEK 12

November 24, 2013
Gillette Stadium – Foxboro, MA

Teams	1st	2nd	3rd	4th	OT	Total
Denver Broncos	17	7	0	7	0	31
New England Patriots	0	0	21	10	3	34

GAME SUMMARY

Hyped as one of the biggest matchups of the year, and rightly so, the 9-1 Broncos were on the road facing the 8-2 New England Patriots. It was also touted as Manning vs. Brady: 2 of the game's all-time best quarterbacks facing off on the gridiron. This contest was expected to be an exciting battle, and despite early indications, it did not disappoint.

Being the Broncos' second high-profile game in a row, the pressure had to be high. Modern NFL doesn't just present challenges on the field, but also intrusive and overexposed media attention along with travel stresses, which inevitably effect performance on the field.

The first half was a complete Denver blowout of the Patriots. In the first quarter alone, Denver scored 17 unanswered points, and they put up another 7 points in the second quarter. At the end of the half, New England was shut out 24-0.

Coming out of the half, the Patriots and Tom Brady were on fire scoring 3 unanswered touchdowns in the third quarter, bringing the game to 24-21 and within 3 points of tying the Broncos. The fourth quarter was a close battle as Denver put up a touchdown, and New England scored both a touchdown and a field goal to tie things up at 31, sending the game into a very unexpected overtime.

In what was considered one of the biggest comeback games of the year, the Patriots clinched the victory when Stephen Gostkowski kicked a 31-yard field goal.

On defense, Denver had a great deal of trouble stopping Julian Edelman and Rob Gronkowski, who combined caught for 300 yards and 3 touchdowns.

Denver's offense relied heavily on Knowshon Moreno, who carried the ball 37 times for a remarkable 224 yards and 1 touchdown.

Despite throwing 2 touchdown passes, Manning had one of his worst performances of this great season. He only passed for 150 yards on 19 of 36 passes with an interception and a 52.78 completion percentage. He was sacked twice for a loss of 18 yards.

His counterpart, Tom Brady, had a much better day passing for 344 yards on 34 of 50 passes with 3 touchdowns and 0 interceptions. While Brady had the better stats for the day, Manning would have better yardage and TD stats on the season than any quarterback in history.

TEAM LEADERS

Passing

Peyton Manning #18
150 Yards, 2 Touchdowns, 1 Interception
(19/36, 52.78 Comp %)

Rushing

Knowshon Moreno #27
224 Yards on 37 Carries
6.05 Yards per Carry
1 Rushing Touchdown

Montee Ball #28
40 Yards on 7 Carries
5.71 Yards per Carry
0 Rushing Touchdowns

Receiving

Jacob Tamme #84
47 Yards on 5 Receptions
9.40 Yards per Reception
1 Touchdown Reception

Demaryius Thomas #88
41 Yards on 4 Receptions
10.25 Yards per Reception
1 Touchdown Reception
Wes Welker #83
31 Yards on 4 Receptions
7.75 Yards per Reception
0 Touchdown Reception

Montee Ball #28
17 Yards on 3 Receptions
5.67 Yards per Reception
0 Touchdown Receptions

Kicking

Matt Prater #5
7 Points Total
1/1 Field Goals
4/4 Extra Points

Interceptions

MANNING CANNON COUNT

IN PURSUIT OF HISTORY

41 | 4,125

TOUCHDOWNS | YARDS

AFTER 12 GAMES

THE BOTTOM LINE

THE BOTTOM LINE

9 - 2

WEEK 13

December 1, 2013
Arrowhead Stadium – Kansas City, MO

Teams	1st	2nd	3rd	4th	Total
Denver Broncos	0	14	14	7	**35**
Kansas City Chiefs	7	14	0	7	**28**

GAME SUMMARY

For the second week in a row, the Broncos were on the road against a tough, playoff-bound opponent. Coming off their second loss of the season, The Broncos not only had something to prove when they met the Kansas City Chiefs, but they also had concerns about locking up the coveted #1 seed in the post season.

Led by quarterback Alex Smith, the Chiefs had only lost to the Chargers in Week 12 and to the Broncos the week before that. Critics of the Chiefs would argue that while their record of 9-2 was quite impressive, that of the 9 teams they defeated only 1 of them would make it to the playoffs (the Eagles, who would be defeated by the New Orleans Saints in the first round wild card game). In short, critics were saying the Chiefs played remarkably well against poorly performing teams. Their only true tests were their losses in the past two weeks when they faced the Broncos and the Chargers.

During the first half of this game, the Chiefs seemed to have proven their critics wrong. After 1 quarter, the Broncos had been shut down, and Kansas City was up by a touchdown. In the second quarter, Denver got on the scoreboard with 2 touchdowns, but the Chiefs kept pace scoring 2 more TDs of their own. At the half, KC was up by 7 points.

Coming out of halftime, the Broncos scored 2 unanswered touchdowns in the 3rd quarter, taking the lead. Both teams would swap touchdowns in the 4th quarter, giving Denver the 7-point victory.

Peyton Manning had another 400+ yard passing game, gaining 403 yards on 22 of 35 passes for 5 touchdowns and 2 interceptions. While Manning was throwing more interceptions than he was earlier in the season, he was still leading his team to victory against a tough opponent and throwing more than twice as many TDs as interceptions.

Montee Ball had his turn as the top rusher, taking 13 carries for 117 yards. Eric Decker was definitely Manning's favorite target as he caught 8 passes for a whopping 174 yards and 4 touchdowns. Demaryius Thomas also received for just over 100 yards on 3 receptions, including one, long 77-yard catch. Knowshon Moreno did not get his usual rushing yardage in this contest, but he did catch 4 passes for 72 yards and a touchdown.

TEAM LEADERS

Passing

Peyton Manning #18
403 Yards, 5 Touchdowns, 2 Interceptions
(22/35, 62.86 Comp %)

Rushing

Montee Ball #28
117 Yards on 13 Carries
9.00 Yards per Carry
0 Rushing Touchdowns

Knowshon Moreno #27
18 Yards on 15 Carries
1.20 Yards per Carry
0 Rushing Touchdown

Receiving

Eric Decker #87
174 Yards on 8 Receptions
21.75 Yards per Reception
4 Touchdown Receptions

Demaryius Thomas #88
106 Yards on 3 Receptions
35.33 Yards per Reception
0 Touchdown Receptions

Knowshon Moreno #27
72 Yards on 4 Receptions
18.00 Yards per Reception
1 Touchdown Reception

Wes Welker #83
38 Yards on 3 Receptions
12.67 Yards per Reception
0 Touchdown Receptions

Kicking

Matt Prater #5
5 Points Total
0/0 Field Goals
5/5 Extra Points

Interceptions

Wesley Woodyard #52
1 Interception

MANNING CANNON COUNT

IN PURSUIT OF HISTORY

41 | 4,125

TOUCHDOWNS | YARDS

AFTER 12 GAMES

THE BOTTOM LINE

10 - 2

WEEK 14

December 8, 2013
Sports Authority Field – Mile High, Denver, CO

Teams	1st	2nd	3rd	4th	Total
Tennessee Titans	14	7	7	0	28
Denver Broncos	10	10	14	17	51

GAME SUMMARY

With twice as many victories as their opponent, the 10-2 Denver Broncos met the 5-7 Tennessee Titans, leaving very few to expect anything but an easy blowout game for Peyton Manning and company, especially with it being a home game after 2 weeks on the road.

With that in mind, the first half was a bit of a shock to the sports world. The Titans jumped out to an early lead, ending the first quarter 14-10. Denver punched back in the second quarter, narrowing Tennessee's lead down to 1 point, trailing the Titans 20-21.

As has happened frequently this year, Manning and the offense came out gunning after halftime. In the 3rd quarter, they outscored the titans, 2 touchdowns to 1. In the 4th quarter, they completely dominated the Titans 17-0, creating a final score of 51-28.

This was another 4-touchdown day for Peyton Manning, who also threw for 397 yards and 0 interceptions on 39 of 59 passes for a 66.10 completion ratio.

On the ground for Denver, Moreno and Ball turned in nearly identical performances of 78 yards on 14 carries for a touchdown (Moreno) and 77 yards on 15 carries for another touchdown (Ball).

Eric Decker was once again Manning's favorite receiver catching 8 passes for 117 yards and a TD. Next up was Demaryius Thomas with 88 yards on 7 catches and a touchdown. Wes Welker and Julius Thomas also caught passes in the end zone.

Some of the biggest news of the day came from the record-shattering, 64-yard field goal from the foot of kicker Matt Prater. The previous record was a 4-way tie between Tom Dempsey, Jason Elam, Sebastian Janikowski, and David Akers. While 3 others had matched Tom Dempsey's 63-yard field goal record set in 1970, it took 44 years for someone to surpass it. While it is said that kickers unfortunately are often overlooked in football as long as they're making their shots and are only noticed when they miss, this was a tremendous feat that should be honored and respected.

TEAM LEADERS

Passing

Peyton Manning #18
397 Yards, 4 Touchdowns, 0 Interceptions
(39/59, 66.10 Comp %)

Rushing

Knowshon Moreno #27
78 Yards on 14 Carries
5.57 Yards per Carry
1 Rushing Touchdown

Montee Ball #28
77 Yards on 15 Carries
5.13 Yards per Carry
1 Rushing Touchdown

Receiving

Eric Decker #87
117 Yards on 8 Receptions
14.63 Yards per Reception
1 Touchdown Reception

Demaryius Thomas #88
88 Yards on 7 Receptions
12.57 Yards per Reception
1 Touchdown Reception

Wes Welker #83
61 Yards on 5 Receptions
12.20 Yards per Reception
1 Touchdown Reception

Jacob Tamme #84
47 Yards on 4 Receptions
11.75 Yards per Reception
0 Touchdown Receptions

Julius Thomas #80
35 Yards on 5 Receptions
7.00 Yards per Reception
1 Touchdown Reception

Knowshon Moreno #27
31 Yards on 6 Receptions
5.17 Yards per Reception
0 Touchdown Receptions

Kicking

Matt Prater #5
15 Points Total
3/3 Field Goals
6/6 Extra Points

Interceptions

Terrance Knighton #94
1 Interception

MANNING CANNON COUNT

IN PURSUIT OF HISTORY

45 | 4,522
TOUCHDOWNS | YARDS

AFTER 13 GAMES

THE BOTTOM LINE

11 - 2

WEEK 15

December 12, 2013
Sports Authority Field – Mile High, Denver CO

Teams	1st	2nd	3rd	4th	Total
San Diego Chargers	3	14	7	3	27
Denver Broncos	10	0	0	10	20

GAME SUMMARY

After beating the Titans the previous week by 23 points, and facing a seemingly outmatched Chargers, who were struggling to avoid a losing season at 6-7, very few expected this to be a challenging game for the 11-2 Broncos.

Besides the overall record, Denver had already beaten the Chargers on the road. Now they were facing them at home just 5 weeks later. The advantage again seemed to clearly reside with the Broncos.

This was a true example of the cliché "any given Sunday."

The last time these teams met, it was also a close game, one in which the Broncos beat the Chargers by 8 points, potentially a 1-score game. In this contest the Chargers would beat the Broncos by 7 points, another 1-score game.

Denver's game was split into bookends, both a 1st and a 4th quarter with a touchdown and field goal in each, while being shutout in the quarters in-between. Those 2 shutout quarters, in which the Chargers scored 21 unanswered points, were really the key to their victory.

Peyton Manning had one of his lower statistical days throwing for 289 yards on 27 of 41 passes for a completion percentage of 65.85, 2 touchdowns, and 1 interception, while being sacked once. Those numbers were better than his counterparts', however, as Philip Rivers only threw for 166 yards on 12 of 20 passes for a 60% completion ratio, 2 touchdowns, and 0 interceptions, while being sacked twice. Other than Manning's one interception, he had a far superior performance than the competition he lost to.

Both team's kickers were flawless, scoring 8 and 9 points each.

So where was this game lost then?

#1 - San Diego rushed for 177 yards and 1 touchdown, while Denver's running game was held to only 18 yards and 0 touchdowns.

#2 - 3rd Down Conversions played a big role in this game too, as the Chargers were successful in 6 of 12 attempts and Denver only converted on 2 of 9 attempts.

#3 - Lastly, losing the turnover battle even just 1-0 is hard to overcome in a close game.

In the 2013 regular season, the Broncos and Chargers split their 2 contests, oddly with each winning on the other's home turf.

TEAM LEADERS

Passing

Peyton Manning #18
289 Yards, 2 Touchdowns, 1 Interception
(27/41, 65.85 Comp %)

Rushing

Knowshon Moreno #27
19 Yards on 8 Carries
2.38 Yards per Carry
0 Rushing Touchdowns

Montee Ball #28
-1 Yards on 3 Carries
-0.33 Yards per Carry
0 Rushing Touchdowns

Receiving

Andre Caldwell #12
59 Yards on 6 Receptions
9.83 Yards per Reception
2 Touchdown Receptions

Montee Ball #28
49 Yards on 5 Receptions
9.80 Yards per Reception
0 Touchdown Receptions

Julius Thomas #80
49 Yards on 4 Receptions
12.25 Yards per Reception
0 Touchdown Receptions

Demaryius Thomas #88
45 Yards on 4 Receptions
11.25 Yards per Reception
0 Touchdown Receptions

Eric Decker #87
42 Yards on 2 Receptions
21.00 Yards per Reception
0 Touchdown Receptions

Knowshon Moreno #27
36 Yards on 5 Receptions
7.20 Yards per Reception
0 Touchdown Receptions

Kicking

Matt Prater #5
8 Points Total
2/2 Field Goals
2/2 Extra Points

Interceptions

None

MANNING CANNON COUNT

IN PURSUIT OF HISTORY

47 | **4,811**

TOUCHDOWNS | YARDS

AFTER 14 GAMES

THE BOTTOM LINE

11 - 3

WEEK 16

December 22, 2013
Reliant Stadium – Houston, TX

Teams	1st	2nd	3rd	4th	Total
Denver Broncos	3	13	0	21	37
Houston Texans	3	3	7	0	13

GAME SUMMARY

Despite starting off the year 2-0, including a hard-fought victory over the post-season-bound San Diego Chargers, the Houston Texans fell remarkably into a terrible winless streak, leaving them to face the Denver Broncos at home with a paltry 2-12 record.

While the final score surprised no one, the road to it had a few unexpected moments. At the half, the score was 16-6 in favor of the Broncos. However, at the end of the 3rd quarter, the Texans had closed the gap to only 3 points with a score of 16-13. Certainly no one would have predicted the team with one of the worst records in all of football trailing the team with one of the best records in all of football by only 3 points with only 1 quarter left to go.

Fortunately for Broncos fans, the 4th quarter went as most would have predicted. Denver scored 3 unanswered touchdowns, while preventing Houston from getting on the scoreboard again.

The final score was 37-13, which translates to a 24-point road victory for the Broncos. That's a good game, even against the worst performing team in football.

Peyton Manning threw for an even 400 yards on 32 of 51 passes for 4 touchdowns and 0 interceptions, and he was sacked once. That equaled a 62.75 completion percentage. It was also a return to unbelievable form as he threw for 4 TDs without giving up a single interception. That was a great sign coming off a loss with the playoffs right around the corner.

In the air, Eric Decker was the team's strongest receiver with 131 yards and 2 touchdowns, followed closely behind by Demaryius Thomas with 123 yards and 1 touchdown.

TEAM LEADERS

Passing

Peyton Manning #18
400 Yards, 4 Touchdowns, 0 Interceptions
(32/51, 62.75 Comp %)

Rushing

Knowshon Moreno #27
76 Yards on 11 Carries
6.91 Yards per Carry
0 Rushing Touchdowns

Montee Ball #28
32 Yards on 4 Carries
8.00 Yards per Carry
0 Rushing Touchdowns

Receiving

Eric Decker #87
131 Yards on 10 Receptions
13.10 Yards per Reception
2 Touchdown Receptions

Demaryius Thomas #88
123 Yards on 8 Receptions
15.38 Yards per Reception
1 Touchdown Reception

Julius Thomas #80
78 Yards on 6 Receptions
13.00 Yards per Reception
1 Touchdown Reception

Knowshon Moreno #27
26 Yards on 2 Receptions
13.00 Yards per Reception
0 Touchdown Receptions

Jacob Tamme #84
22 Yards on 3 Receptions
7.33 Yards per Reception
0 Touchdown Receptions

Kicking

Matt Prater #5
7 Points Total
2/3 Field Goals
1/1 Extra Points

Interceptions

Patrick Willis #52
1 Interception

MANNING CANNON COUNT

IN PURSUIT OF HISTORY

51 | 5,211
TOUCHDOWNS | **YARDS**

AFTER 15 GAMES

THE BOTTOM LINE

12 - 3

WEEK 17

December 29, 2013
O.co Oakland Coliseum – Oakland, CA

Teams	1st	2nd	3rd	4th	Total
Denver Broncos	14	17	0	3	**34**
Oakland Raiders	0	0	0	14	**14**

GAME SUMMARY

No one expected this to be a difficult game or even a close one. The Oakland Raiders struggled heavily in 2013, coming into the game at 3-12, an exact mirror image of the Broncos' 12-3 record. What was on the minds' of football fans everywhere was if Peyton Manning would set the all-time, single season passing record of which he was within a meager 265 yards of shattering.

The current record was held by Drew Brees at 5,476 yards in 2011. In just the first half, Manning threw 28 passes for 25 completions and 266 yards, ending the season with 5,477 passing yards and a new record. His completion percentage while accomplishing this was an astounding 89.29.

Manning played for 2 quarters, securing not only his record but the #1 seed for the playoffs.

Backup quarterback Brock Osweiler saw some action when Manning came out of the game, going 9 for 13 for 85 yards while being sacked twice.

The rushing game was solid with 124 yards total, 72 of those on the legs of Montee Ball. The receiving game accounted for all 4 touchdowns and 351 yards, led by Demaryius Thomas who had 113 yards and 2 touchdowns on 6 catches.

TEAM LEADERS

Passing

Peyton Manning #18
266 Yards, 4 Touchdowns, 0 Interceptions
(25/28, 89.29 Comp %)

Brock Osweiler #17
85 Yards, 0 Touchdowns, 0 Interceptions
(9/13, 69.23 Comp %)

Rushing

Montee Ball #28
72 Yards on 10 Carries
7.20 Yards per Carry
0 Rushing Touchdowns

Ronnie Hillman #21
30 Yards on 12 Carries
2.50 Yards per Carry
0 Rushing Touchdowns

Knowshon Moreno #27
23 Yards on 6 Carries
3.83 Yards per Carry
1 Rushing Touchdown

Receiving

Demaryius Thomas #88
113 Yards on 6 Receptions
18.83 Yards per Reception
2 Touchdown Receptions

Andre Caldwell #12
42 Yards on 3 Receptions
14.00 Yards per Reception
0 Touchdown Receptions

Knowshon Moreno #27
41 Yards on 5 Receptions
8.20 Yards per Reception
1 Touchdown Reception

Julius Thomas #80
36 Yards on 5 Receptions
7.20 Yards per Reception
0 Touchdown Receptions

Eric Decker #87
27 Yards on 4 Receptions
6.75 Yards per Reception
1 Touchdown Reception

Kicking

Matt Prater #5
10 Points Total
2/2 Field Goals
4/4 Extra Points

Interceptions

Tarell Brown #25
1 Interception

Manning Cannon Count

In Pursuit of History

55	5,477
Touchdowns	**Yards**

After **16** Games

The Bottom Line

13 - 3

REGULAR SEASON WRAP UP

The regular season ended with some impressive stats for many Broncos' players. Here are the leaders in key categories:

Regular Season Rushing: Knowshon Moreno finished the year with 1,038 rushing yards and 10 touchdowns. The next leading rusher was Montee Ball who ran for 559 yards and 4 touchdowns. The third leading rusher was Ronnie Hillman who put up 218 yards and 1 touchdown. The only other Broncos player to run in a touchdown was Peyton Manning, who ran in a 1-yarder.

Regular Season Receiving: With Peyton Manning setting the NFL season passing record, one would assume the Broncos' receivers would have to have some impressive numbers, and you'd of course be correct. Demaryius Thomas was the team receiving leader with 1,430 yards on 92 catches for 14 touchdowns. Eric Decker was next in line with 1,288 yards on 87 grabs for 11 touchdowns.

Besides the 2 players with 1,000+ receiving yards, there were 2 other players with 750+ yard seasons (Julius Thomas with 788 yards and 12 touchdowns; and Wes Welker with 778 yards and 10 touchdowns.) And, that's still not where it ends, as running back Knowshon Moreno caught 60 passes for 548 yards and 3 touchdowns.

Regular Season All-Purpose Yards: Knowshon Moreno contributed heavily to the Broncos' offense all season long. His total receiving and rushing assault racked up 1,586 yards and 13 touchdowns.

Trindon Holliday accounted for 1,053 all-purpose yards, including an 81-yard punt return for a TD and a 105-yard kick return for a TD. 775 of his yards came on kick returns, and 271 additional yards came on punt returns.

Regular Season Defense: Danny Trevathan was the defensive leader with 128 tackles, 2 sacks, and 3 interceptions. Wesley Woodyard was next up with 84 tackles, 1.5 sacks, and 1 interception. Chris Harris also had 3 interceptions on the year, along with 60 tackles.

Shaun Phillips was the sack leader with 10, along with 1 interception. Malik Jackson was second in sacks with 6.

2 defensive touchdowns were scored. Von Miller ran a fumble back for a touchdown, and Dominique Rodgers-Cromartie ran an interception back for a touchdown.

Regular Season Kicking: Matt Prater was nearly perfect all year, hitting 25 of 26 field goals (longest 64 yards, which was an NFL record) and 75 of 75 field goals. In fact, the only field goal Prater missed was a shot from over 50 yards away. In all of the NFL in 2013, Prater was #2 in Points Scored with 150, #1 in extra points made and attempted with 75 in both categories, and he was #1 in Field Goal % with 96.15%. For his impressive efforts, Prater went to the Pro Bowl. The 150 points he contributed to the Broncos certainly was instrumental in their fantastic season.

Regular Season Team Rankings: Denver ended the season with a record of 13-3, which was an .813 win percentage, scoring 606 points of their own (1st of all 32 NFL Teams), while only allowing 399 points by opponents. That obviously put them as the #1 team in the AFC, which was 2 games above the Kansas City Chiefs. What also clearly put Denver above Kansas City was that they scored 176 more points, while only allowing 94 more points (that equals Denver outscoring their opponents by 82 more points than the Chiefs outscored their opponents).

WEEK 19

Divisional Championship - January 12, 2014
Sports Authority Field – Mile High, Denver, CO

Teams	1st	2nd	3rd	4th	Total
San Diego Chargers	0	0	0	17	**17**
Denver Broncos	7	7	3	7	**24**

GAME SUMMARY

On January 12, 2014, the San Diego Chargers traveled to Sports Authority Field to meet the Denver Broncos in the Divisional Championship Game.

For the first 3 quarters of this playoff encounter, the Chargers were completely shutout. In fact, Philip Rivers was not able to get much of anything going in this game until the 4th quarter, in which he rallied his team to score 17 points. Fortunately for Denver fans, it was just too little too late to overcome the Broncos' established lead. Although the Chargers made it a 1-score game in the end (as their past 2 contests have also been), the Broncos never lost their lead at any point in this game.

Despite having this game seemingly well-in-hand the entire time, the Broncos did lose the turnover war 2-0 with a Peyton Manning interception and Julius Thomas's lost fumble.

The defense certainly had a great day, shutting down the Chargers for 3 straight quarters and sacking Philip Rivers 4 times for a loss of 23 yards.

While Peyton Manning did not have one of his best games of the year against the Chargers, winning, not statistics, is the name of the game in the playoffs. With 230 yards passing, 2 TDs, and 1 Interception, it was one of Manning's lowest performing games.

Matt Prater was 1 for 2 on field goals in this game, which was a little odd because he had only missed one other field goal all year.

In uncharacteristic fashion, none of Denver's rushers or receivers had more than 100 on the day. The leader was Knowshon Moreno, who rushed for 82 yards and a touchdown. Even if you count his 12 receiving yards, his total would be 94, just shy of 100. The second-leading rusher was Montee Ball who had 52 yards on 10 runs.

In the air, Julius Thomas had the most yardage with 76 on 6 catches. Demaryius Thomas was next in line with 54 yards and a touchdown on 8 catches. Wes Welker also caught a touchdown and 38 yards on 6 passes.

TEAM LEADERS

Passing

Peyton Manning #18
230 Yards, 2 Touchdowns, 1 Interception
(25/36, 69.44 Comp %)

Rushing

Knowshon Moreno #27
82 Yards on 23 Carries
3.57 Yards per Carry
1 Rushing Touchdown

Montee Ball #28
52 Yards on 10 Carries
5.20 Yards per Carry
0 Rushing Touchdowns

Receiving

Julius Thomas #80
76 Yards on 6 Receptions
12.67 Yards per Reception
0 Touchdown Receptions

Demaryius Thomas #88
54 Yards on 8 Receptions
6.75 Yards per Reception
1 Touchdown Reception

Wes Welker #83
38 Yards on 6 Receptions
6.33 Yards per Reception
1 Touchdown Reception

Eric Decker #87
32 Yards on 2 Receptions
16.00 Yards per Reception
0 Touchdown Receptions

Knowshon Moreno #27
12 Yards on 1 Receptions
12.00 Yards per Reception
0 Touchdown Receptions

Kicking

Matt Prater #5
6 Points Total
1/2 Field Goals
3/3 Extra Points

Interceptions

None

THE BOTTOM LINE

14 - 3

WEEK 20

AFC Championship Game - January 19, 2014
Sports Authority Field – Mile High, Denver, CO

Teams	1st	2nd	3rd	4th	Total
New England Patriots	0	3	0	13	**16**
Denver Broncos	3	10	7	6	**26**

GAME SUMMARY

The AFC Championship Game saw the New England Patriots on the road facing the Denver Broncos. Both teams performed nearly equally during the regular season, with the Patriots finishing 12-4, just trailing behind the Broncos's better record of 13-3.

The Patriots had one less victory during the regular season, but they did beat the Broncos in an overtime thriller earlier in the season. However, that game was a Patriot home game on the East Coast. This playoff encounter would take place in Mile High, a welcoming home game for the Broncos.

This was to be the high-intensity rematch of Broncos vs. Pats, Manning vs. Brady, with the winner making it to the big game and with the loser getting an early start on the pre-season.

Coming off a solid but unspectacular week against the Chargers, Peyton Manning put up great numbers in this contest, throwing for 400 yards on the button, 2 touchdowns, and 0 interceptions on 32 of 43 passes for a 74.42 completion %.

While Brady was sacked twice for a loss of 21 yards and Manning was not sacked at all, Brady simply did not have as good of a day as Manning. He threw for 277 yards, 1 touchdown, and 0 interceptions on 24 of 38 passes (a 63.16 completion %).

If there were any legitimate criticisms of the previous week's victory, it would be that the Broncos let the Chargers, a team not likely to make it to the Super Bowl much less win it, come within one score of tying the game. If that criticism were valid (after all a win is a win, and this is the NFL), the Broncos crushed that complaint this week. There was no denying that Tom Brady and the 2nd-seed Patriots at 12-4 were a team very capable of beating anyone in the NFL. The Broncos won this game by a score and a field goal, not leaving their opponent the possibility of a last minute drive to win the game.

Both teams had solid ball control, neither giving up a single turnover.

On the ground, Denver put up 107 yards and 0 touchdowns, with Moreno carrying the bulk of it at 59 yards.

On the receiving end, Thomas & Thomas were the two leaders. Demaryius Thomas was at the top of the hill with 134 yards and 1 touchdown on 7 receptions, the longest of which was for 30 yards. Julius Thomas also had a good day catching 8 passes for 85 yards.

The Broncos looked strong in this performance, outscoring the Patriots in every quarter but the last, and all they needed to do in that quarter was to run the clock out. They may have very well been able to outscore the Patriots in the 4th quarter too if the score had necessitated the risk.

Team Leaders

Passing

Peyton Manning #18
400 Yards, 1 Touchdown, 0 Interceptions
(32/43, 74.42 Comp %)

Rushing

Knowshon Moreno #27
59 Yards on 14 Carries
4.21 Yards per Carry
0 Rushing Touchdowns

Montee Ball #28
43 Yards on 12 Carries
3.58 Yards per Carry
0 Rushing Touchdowns

Receiving

Demaryius Thomas #88
134 Yards on 7 Receptions
19.14 Yards per Reception
1 Touchdown Reception

Julius Thomas #80
85 Yards on 8 Receptions
10.63 Yards per Reception
0 Touchdown Receptions

Eric Decker #87
73 Yards on 5 Receptions
14.60 Yards per Reception
0 Touchdown Receptions

Wes Welker #83

38 Yards on 4 Receptions
9.50 Yards per Reception
0 Touchdown Receptions

Jacob Tamme #84
24 Yards on 2 Receptions
12.00 Yards per Reception
1 Touchdown Reception

Knowshon Moreno #27
22 Yards on 2 Receptions
11.00 Yards per Reception
0 Touchdown Receptions

Kicking

Matt Prater #5
14 Points Total
4/4 Field Goals
2/2 Extra Points

Interceptions

None

THE BOTTOM LINE

15 - 3

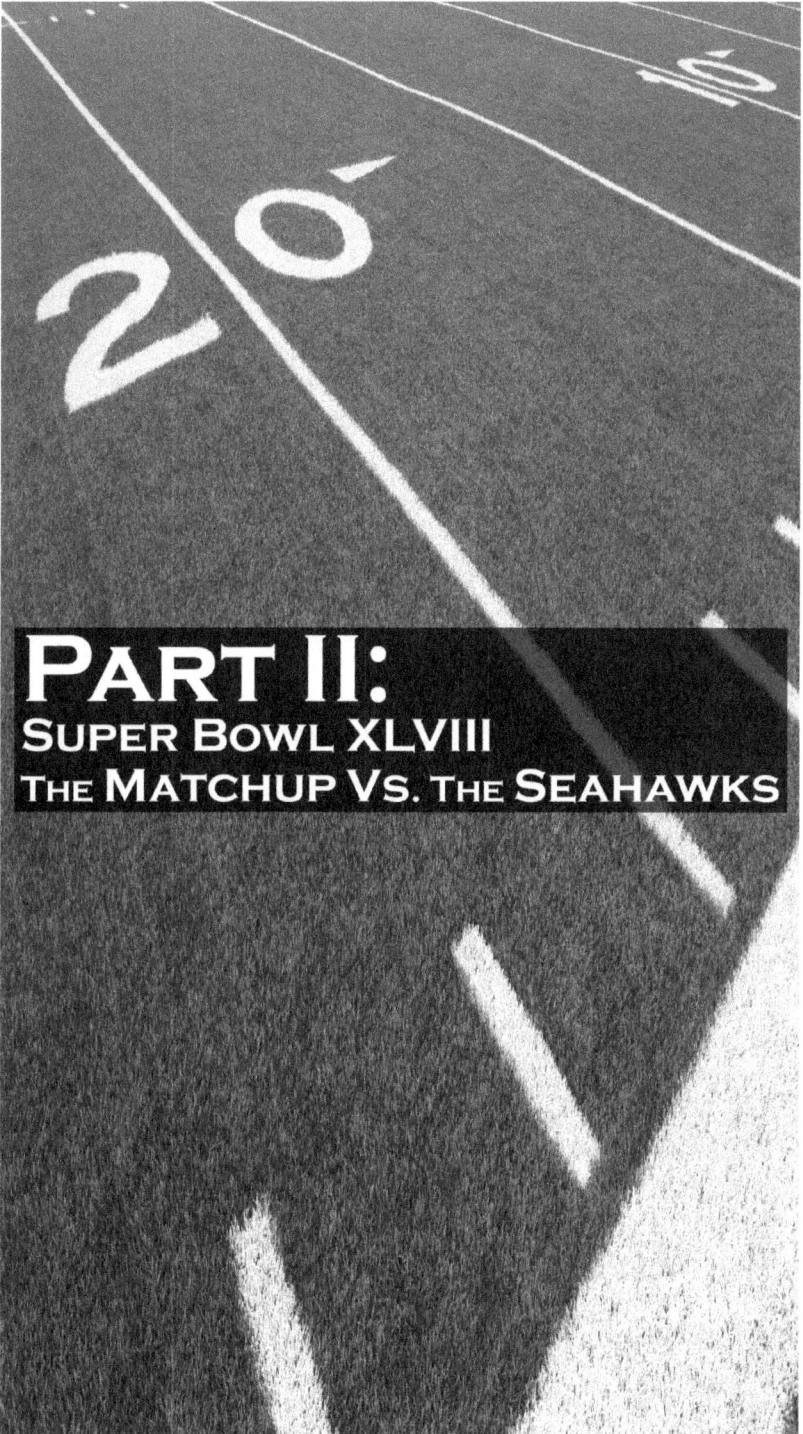

PART II:
SUPER BOWL XLVIII
THE MATCHUP VS. THE SEAHAWKS

PEYTON MANNING 98

THE
SUPER BOWL
XLVIII
MATCHUP

In the regular season, the Denver Broncos were 13-3, and the Seattle Seahawks were also 13-3. While the overall records were similar, the teams have very different strengths. Here are some key stats on how they both battled their way to the big game, side-by-side for a direct comparison.

POINTS SCORED VS.
POINTS ALLOWED

TEAM	Points Scored	Points Allowed	Points Differential
Broncos	606	399	+207
Seahawks	417	231	+186

Spreading those numbers out over the 16 games each team played in the regular season, that works out to be:

The Broncos beat their opponents in 2013 by an average of 12.94 points.

The Seahawks bear their opponents in 2013 by an average of 11.63 points.

That is an advantage of 1.31 points in favor of the Denver Broncos.

TEAM PASSING STATISTICS

TEAM	Comp	Attempts	Comp %	Yards	TDs	Inter-Ceptions
Broncos	461	675	68.30%	5,444	55	10
Seahawks	267	420	63.57%	3,236	27	9

While Russell Wilson did a great job leading the Seahawks through an impressive season all the way to the Super Bowl, his 2013 numbers were not even in the same league as those of Peyton Manning.

Manning unsurprisingly bested Wilson in every category. One of the numbers to take into consideration that will likely come into play in the Super Bowl is that Wilson's touchdown to interception ratio is 3:1. Manning's TD to INT ratio is 5.5:1, which is nearly double that of his counterpart. In other words, Wilson is almost twice as likely to throw an interception per touchdown as Manning.

If the Broncos can pass successfully against the Seahawks' defense, there should not be much of a chance for Wilson and the Seahawks offense to match their production. The Seahawks passing game simply cannot compete. They'll have to try to win with running and defense.

TEAM RUSHING STATISTICS

TEAM	Carries	Yards	Average	Touchdowns
Broncos	461	1,873	4.06 Yards	16
Seahawks	509	2,188	4.30 Yards	14

The rushing numbers were also not too far apart. People have been fast to point out that Seattle has rushed for 315 more yards. While that it was true (Seahawks 2,188 rushing to Broncos 1,873), they took 48 more carries to do it. The average per carry rushing attempt was very similar with the Seahawks only running for .24 of yard more on each of those carries. However, that .24 advantage does reside with the Seahawks, and sometimes drives and even games are settled by inches.

On 48 less running plays, the Broncos scored 2 more rushing touchdowns than the Seahawks. So, the broncos clearly have better ability to run the ball in to the end zone.

DEFENSIVE TAKE-AWAYS

TEAM	Interceptions	Forced Fumbles
Broncos	17	9
Seahawks	28	20

The Seahawks clearly have an advantage when it comes to taking the ball away from the other team's offense, both in the air and on the ground.

TEAM KICKING STATISTICS

TEAM	Extra Points	Extra Point %	Field Goals Made	Field Goals Attempted	Field Goal %	Total Points
Broncos	75	100%	25	26	96.15%	150
Seahawks	44	100%	33	35	94.29%	143

The kicking stats are very close. While the Broncos have more total points and a slightly better field goal percentage, the Seahawks have kicked more field goals with a similar success ratio.

For the Broncos, Matt Prater was a 2013 Pro Bowl Kicker who set the 64-yard NFL field goal record this year. For Seattle, 2013 has been the best year so far in Steven Hauschka's career. In past years, Hauschka has had significantly lower field goal percentages, and he has also missed two extra points in 2012 and another in 2009. It can also be said that Prater was having a career year in 2013, but he last missed an extra point in 2010. One of Hauschka's missed field goals in 2013 came at less than 30 yards away, and his longest field goal was from 53 yards away. The long kicking game is definitely in favor of Prater and the Broncos. The shorter kicking game is going to be close, with maybe a slight advantage again to Prater and the Broncos.

College Stats

Year	G	Comp	Att	Comp %	Yards	TD	INT	Rate
1994	11	89	144	61.8	1141	11	6	145.2
1995	11	244	380	64.2	2954	22	4	146.5
1996	11	243	380	63.9	3287	20	12	147.7
1997	12	287	477	60.2	3819	36	11	147.7
Career	45	863	1381	62.5	11201	89	33	147.1

Despite his impressive collegiate career, which led to a #1 overall draft pick to the Indianapolis Colts, Manning never led the NCAA in passing yards and touchdowns as he would later do in the NFL. The closest he came to leading the NCAA in passing yards was when he finished 4th in 1997. For touchdowns, his best was finishing 3rd in all of college football, also in 1997. Those are impressive accomplishments, but it does seem odd that the same quarterback who led the professional ranks on many occasions never once led the collegiate ranks. One could conclude that Manning has improved with experience and/or that he has been surrounded by better athletes in the pro ranks.

In fact, Peyton never led the NCAA in any of the major categories. He did, however, lead the SEC in pass completions with 243 in 1996, pass attempts with 380 in 1996, completion percentage with 63.9% in 1996, total yards with 3,789 in 1997, and total yards per play with 7.2 in 1997. They are great accomplishments indeed, but they pale in comparison to his NFL stats that put him into the discussion of greatest pro QB of all time.

In his senior year of 1997, Manning came in second in Heisman Trophy voting to Charles Woodson, edging out quarterback Ryan Leaf and wide receiver Randy Moss. It is important to note that the pros thought Manning was the top talent in all of college football when he was the overall #1 draft pick of 1998. Heisman winner Woodson was picked 4th overall.

Pro Stats:

Year	Team	G	Comp	Att	Cmp %	Yards	TD	INT	FUM	QBR	Rating
1998	Colts	16	326	575	56.7	3,739	26	28	3	--	71.2
1999	Colts	16	331	533	62.1	4,135	26	15	1	--	90.7
2000	Colts	16	357	571	62.5	4,413	33	15	4	--	94.7
2001	Colts	16	343	547	62.7	4,131	26	23	4	--	84.1
2002	Colts	16	392	591	66.3	4,200	27	19	5	--	88.8
2003	Colts	16	379	566	67.0	4,267	29	10	2	--	99.0
2004	Colts	16	336	497	67.6	4,557	49	10	4	--	121.1
2005	Colts	16	305	453	67.3	3,747	28	10	3	--	104.1
2006	Colts	16	362	557	65.0	4,397	31	9	2	87.2	101.0
2007	Colts	16	337	515	65.4	4,040	31	14	6	78.4	98.0
2008	Colts	16	371	555	66.8	4,002	27	12	0	79.3	95.0
2009	Colts	16	393	571	68.8	4,500	33	16	1	82.8	99.9
2010	Colts	16	450	679	66.3	4,700	33	17	2	71.7	91.9
2012	Broncos	16	400	583	68.6	4,659	37	11	2	82.4	105.8
2013	Broncos	16	450	659	68.3	5,477	55	10	5	82.9	115.1
Career		240	5,532	8,452	65.5	64,964	491	219	44	--	97.2

CHECK OUT MORE GREAT RELEASES FROM
MEGALODON ENTERTAINMENT LLC

Follow the **New Orleans Saints** through their amazing **Super Bowl XLIV (44) Championship** season, and re-experience every game, relive every score, and savor every victory.

Travel with The Saints on their long, often trying 43 years on the road to success.

Compare the stats on every Saints Quarterback. Who has the most yards, wins, and completions? Archie Manning, Drew Brees, Bobby Hebert, or Aaron Brooks? Find out which Saints coach has the best record and the most games. Sean Payton, Jim Mora, or Bum Phillips? This book is the perfect companion for new and long-time Saints fans alike.

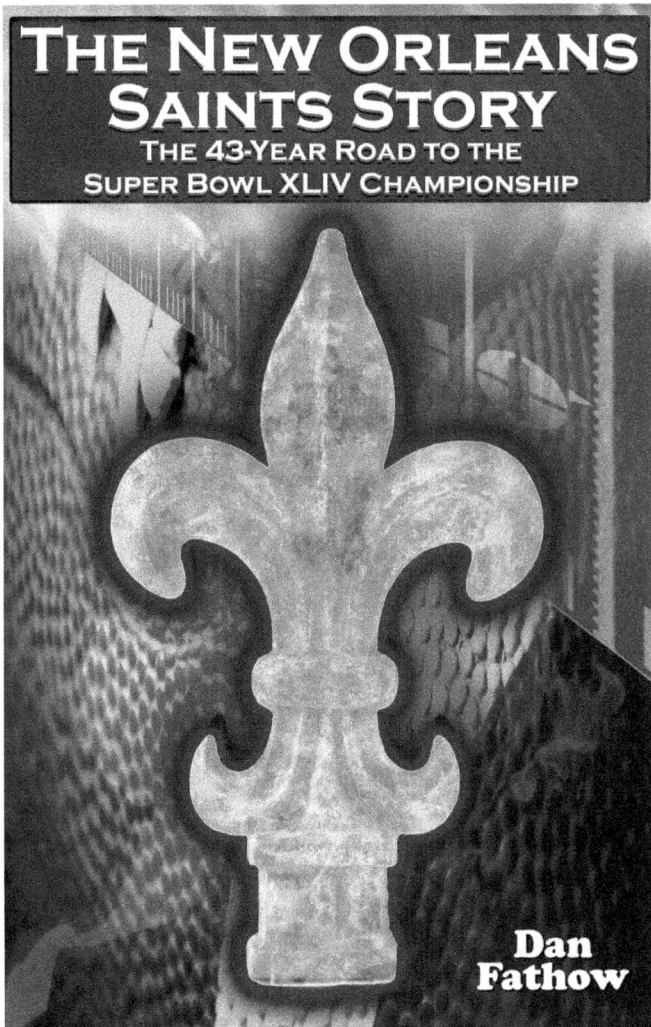

THE NEW ORLEANS SAINTS STORY
THE 43-YEAR ROAD TO THE SUPER BOWL XLIV CHAMPIONSHIP

Dan Fathow

ISBN 978-0-9800605-7-7

The defending BCS national champions, the 2012 Alabama Crimson Tide, dominated opponents throughout the season, earning a repeat trip to the 2013 BCS National Championship Game. Quarterback A.J. McCarron had a stellar year, putting up great numbers and leading his team back to the big game. Legendary coach Nick Saban kept his team focused and playing sharp, smart football all year long, becoming SEC Champions along the way. Follow the Crimson Tide as they destroy opponents, including their rival LSU Tigers and the Georgia Bulldogs in two of the most exciting and most talked about games of the year. Relive the magical 2012 season, victory by victory, quarter by quarter, and score by score all the way to the 2013 BCS National Championship Game against the Notre Dame Fighting Irish.

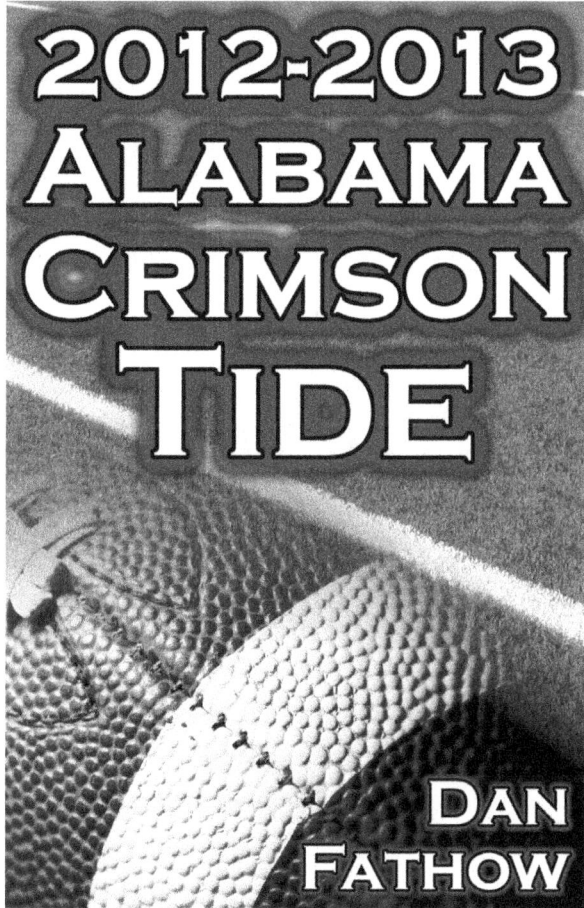

ISBN: 978-1-61589-038-5

www.ingramcontent.com/pod-product-compliance
Lightning Source LLC
Chambersburg PA
CBHW072205090426
42740CB00012B/2391